M000222101

About the Author

Moss Kaplan grew up in Malaysia, New Zealand, Nepal and India. Previous occupations include circus clown and stage carpenter, and currently he teaches creative writing at Denver School of the Arts. He has a BA in Theatre from Lewis and Clark College, a diploma from Circle in the Square Theatre School in New York City, an MA in English Education from The University of Colorado at Boulder, and an MA in Creative Writing from Fairleigh Dickinson University. His creative non-fiction essay "Viewing the Dead," published in "The Literary Review," was a *Notable Essay in The Best American Essays* of 2015. This is his first book. He lives in Denver, Colorado with his wife and two children.

VISIT MOSSKAPLAN.COM

LITTLE
BOUND BOOKS

THE LITTLE BOUND BOOKS ESSAY SERIES

———

OTHER OFFERINGS IN THE SERIES

WWW.LITTLEBOUNDBOOKS.COM

Boy of Mine

An Experiment in Time Travel

Boy of Mine

An Experiment in Time Travel

MOSS KAPLAN

THE LITTLE BOUND BOOKS ESSAY SERIES
WWW.LITTLEBOUNDBOOKS.COM

LITTLE BOUND BOOKS

Small Books. Big Impact | www.littleboundbooks.com

© 2020 Text by Moss Kaplan

Published in 2019 by Homebound Publications
Cover & Interior Designed by Leslie M. Browning
Cover Illustration: © by Varshesh Joshi

ISBN 9781947003798
First Edition Trade Paperback

10 9 8 7 6 5 4 3 2 1

Homebound Publications is committed to ecological stewardship. We greatly value the natural environment and invest in environmental conservation.

dearest Toby,

If you're reading this, it's because I'm dead.

I'm not currently dead, of course—as I write this, I am a healthy forty-seven-year-old man and you've just turned eleven. You've found the padded maroon three-ring binder containing my will filled with a couple hundred pages of impenetrable legalese informing you to share everything straight down the middle with your sister, and since there was an empty section in the binder labeled 'Personal Information', I thought it prudent to include something with a dramatic opening sentence. If I get lucky and die at a reasonable old age, you will be approximately the same age I am now when you finally read this. I like the symmetry of that possibility, especially if you have children, and you're in the throes of trying to be a not-so-terrible parent yourself.

For some mysterious evolutionary reason, children don't want to know much about their parent's past while they're growing up, or at least I didn't. And this is compounded, I imagine, by many parents' reluctance to reveal too much of their lives in the first place, especially if their formative years were miserable or confusing or complicated. Like most childhoods probably, mine was all those things at various moments, but mostly it was just *unusual*— dramatically different from your childhood. Mine was similar perhaps to first-generation immigrants, where the chasm of difference between their own upbringing and that of their American-born children makes talking about the past seem much harder. In my case, the necessary connections are scattered across the globe: born in Cincinnati, then a brief time as a baby in the Philippines, then to a small town on the north island of New Zealand, then to Malaysia for a couple of years, then Kathmandu, Nepal for most of the rest of my childhood; I then spent a year at boarding school in India before moving to the United States for the first time as a teenager. Then Vermont, Colorado, and traveling with Ringling Brothers Circus for a year as a clown before going to college in Oregon; I left college after a year for South

Africa, then returned to finish school and eventually moved to New York City. Then back to Boulder, Colorado where your grandma lives—the closest place I could ever really call home—before settling in Denver at the end of my twenties. You know some of the above, of course, but I don't think you ever knew the chronology. To write all these far-flung places down feels strange even to me, like a dozen separate lives somehow merged into one.

Think of how many times you have visited your mother's childhood home in Ithaca, New York— her whole childhood rooted in that one place. The same roads, houses, neighbors, a coherent landscape of time, place, and memory. Mine is impossible to re-create—jumbled wires pointing in different directions and cultures across several continents. The other day, I was looking online for some decent "icebreaker" questions for my high school students and I came across this one, which made me laugh out loud: *Would you rather run away with the circus, or move to another country alone where you don't speak the language?* Funny, of course, because I did both, and whatever else my life adds up to by the end, I'm reasonably certain that I'm one of a select few who can answer that ridiculous question with any kind of authority.

Your life so far has had the same coherence as your mother's: one house, one town, one elementary school, friends whom you've known since you were a toddler. I am happy about this, although I also sense there is a growing hunger for adventure bubbling in your veins. Increasingly, I must care for you on your own (sometimes complicated) terms, staying out of the way when necessary, and certainly not wrecking your peace of mind by revealing too soon the many hypocrisies and horrors of the grown-up world. This protection was not one I was afforded, and so I am cautious—perhaps overly-so—in wanting to protect you. Recently you heard a gaggle of us adults talking about all the shitbag men in the news these days—powerful men who behave terribly, and mostly get away with it.

"What's a shitbag?" you said.

"Grown up stuff," I replied.

And that was the right thing to say in that moment because I see your job in life right now as mostly focused on solving your Rubik's Cube in under fifty seconds, or making a bullwhip out of rubber bands and string and snapping it a thousand times as you pontificate on the wonders of "breaking the sound barrier," or as of this week, organizing and cataloging the couple hundred books in your bedroom—a tedious task I highly doubt you will ever complete, but admire you nonetheless for the attempt. I spend a lot of time fielding your questions, such as "Why does hot tea cool down to below room temperature?" or "Why does the iron in our blood not react to magnets?" Questions, of course, that I have no answers for. I am driven half-mad sometimes by all your queries, or more often, just left exhausted by always taking an interest. I never want to shut down your curiosity, enthusiasm, or desire just to talk, even if I do occasionally say, "Toby, can we please, please, talk about something else for a while?" Or if I'm really crawling inside my skin, I say, "Toby, sometimes I just need to hear my own thoughts." I am honestly not sure what kids like you used your outsize brains for before the advent of YouTube and Google searches. But mostly, I try to appreciate the fact that you still want to communicate in the first place. In the novel A *Hologram for the King* by Dave Eggers, the main character, Alan, is talking to a Saudi doctor he has befriended. The doctor says:

I'm trying to prevent my son from becoming an asshole like his father. Do you have advice?

—Does he tell you anything? Alan asked.

—Did you tell your mother anything?

Alan had not. Who did young men talk to? Young men have no one to talk to, and even when they do, they don't know what to say or how. And this is why they commit most of the crimes of the world.

I suspect that silence will not be your main problem in life, and I do hope for all this world that you have continued to *talk* into adulthood—by that, I mean expressing your feelings, frustrations, and enthusiasms—and that I played my role in cultivating that part of you. *Listening* is a decent skill too, for the record, and I hope you've learned how to do that as well.

I can hear you asking, "What's the point of this letter, Dad?"

Like children, adults cannot always easily explain their own impulses.

Maybe the letter is just an experiment in time travel, an opportunity for you to reach back across the decades to know your father's heart and mind at a specific moment during your childhood. Or maybe it's far more selfish than that—my way to understand myself and all the conflicting and challenging demands of being a parent. Or maybe it's about our collective identity:

Who am I with you?

Who am I apart from you?

Because it's easy to lose track. Sometimes I feel like little more than the aggregate of my responsibilities: to my family, to my students, to my health, to cooking and shopping and maintaining everything all the time. Just today, I was in the basement changing out a circuit breaker, with you pointing the flashlight in every direction but the one spot I needed the light, while repeatedly saying, "I have a bad feeling about this, Dad." Maybe the letter is just me figuring out what autobiographical information is okay to reveal to my children, and what is best to keep to myself. When I was a young adult, both my mother and father told me things I wish they hadn't—my father once thought it would be a good idea to introduce me to a prostitute he fell in love with when he was living in Zambia while still married to his second wife back in the States. I never really figured out how to integrate this kind of information with the people I wanted my parents to be. A fantasy, perhaps, but one I wish they had let me maintain. Perhaps because of this, I am too cautious about revealing things that might unwittingly traumatize you.

Several weeks ago, the power went out in the evening and the entire neighborhood was plunged into darkness. You were a little nervous about it, and I told you everything would be fine. Your sister was already asleep and your mom was out, so it was just you and me in the black, and you kept asking me when the lights would come back on.

"Soon," I said. "For millennia, this is how everyone lived, so I think we can handle a few minutes."

And then you asked me, "Did this happen a lot when you were a kid in Nepal?" and I told you that it did, several times a week, in fact, and we just learned to live by candlelight, and read books, or simply go to bed a little earlier than usual. You seemed comforted by this, and I was so happy that you had reached across my sprawling time-space continental divide.

As often as you ask about my life, I will answer.

And perhaps as you get older, you will ask more often. Is it possible that over the years ahead, my need for this letter becomes obsolete—a moment comes when I have told you everything, or at least enough, and I can quietly remove it from the three-ring binder? As a teacher, I spend a lot of time around teenagers, so I fear the opposite trajectory: you burrowing down inside your own secret world, and it becomes harder and harder to reach you. Most likely, the years are coming when your mother and I will have to accommodate to a more distant you, but I hope not. Or at the very least, if you do slip further away for a time, you will come back.

By the way, if you're wondering why this letter is not also addressed to your sister, don't assume it's because you're somehow the favored child. The truth is that I usually do prefer one or the other of you, but it changes minute-to-minute. (This morning you were fighting with each other in the car over whether a helium balloon can float into orbit, and the bet was up to a hundred dollars, which neither of you has, and I hated you both equally for a little while, even though you were obviously right about the balloon not being able to reach orbit and you knew it.) No, the simplest reason this letter is solely for you is that you are my son—boy of mine, which I sometimes call you—and because I never had a close relationship with my own father, I want you to know "the real me" in a way that I never knew him.

It's a man-to-man thing, I guess, lame as that sounds when I write it.

Of course, it's fine to share it with Molly, and I plan to write her a separate letter and place it right next to this one in the padded binder—but she is only seven and I need to see what kind of person she becomes and what kind of father I'm going to end up being to her before I write it. I already have a fairly clear idea about your essential nature. Even as a toddler, you had very particular habits of mind. I recently found a video on my laptop of you and me having a conversation when you were three, and aside from your early syntax errors, the tenor of our discussions hasn't changed all that much. You wanted to know why your skin didn't just fall off your bones, and I didn't have a good answer.

Now that my own father is dead, I do wish I knew more about his life—things like what his childhood was like, the moment he knew he wanted to live and raise us in far-flung places like Nepal, his reasons for my parents' divorce, and ultimately why he wasn't a very good father to his own four kids. Then again, writing that sentence, something seems off about it. It certainly sounds right to want answers to those things, but do I really want his acrimonious reasons for divorcing my mother? I think not. If I could snap my fingers and plop Dad down here on the couch in the study where I'm typing, what would I actually want to talk about? His austere Jewish upbringing in Boston? Probably not that either. Maybe I'd just fix us some food—grilled cheese and tomato soup, since it's fall and the leaves are all coming down this week— and we'd chat about whatever—politics and all those shitbag men in the news these days; global warming and how terrified I am that your children's children may not have a sustainable future on this planet; I'd tell him I recently remembered walking on his back when I was little, and now I've started asking you and Molly to do the same to me. His aches and pains have become my aches and pains. Are your kids walking on your back? It's not the history of his life that I long for—it's a feeling of closeness, a connection that I never really felt in any sustained way.

Are you still reading?

Should I have tried to say it all in a paragraph or a page?

Is it still the age of Twitter, when no one wants to really read anything of substance at all? Maybe this letter is just me overcompensating—we are close today, and I hope tomorrow, but what will the future bring? Maybe my job is simply to deliver you to physical and emotional independence and then launch you into the world; maybe as kids we just want to know we are loved and protected and cared for, and it's not more complicated than that. Throw in a few family traditions that you can pass down to your own kids, and call that a successful upbringing.

We certainly don't want our parents' inner lives!

Or do we? I can't decide.

I'm sorry I didn't give you more traditions, by the way, but this was not how I was raised either. All those countries and cultures, and what stuck? Respect for many faiths and customs, but few to call my own. I can barely tolerate Christmas for all the usual disgusting materialistic reasons, but we celebrate it anyway. You never believed in Santa, which I have always admired about you. From a very early age, you told us what you wanted for Christmas, simple as that. And I'm not sorry that I never gave you God. I suspect you may be a scientist of some kind as an adult, so perhaps your godless upbringing was formative in some way.

What will you remember fondly from your childhood?

What will you resent?

What will you forget completely?

As parents we're mostly working in the blind— like you in the basement, pointing the flashlight in all the wrong directions while I try not to electrocute myself. At the very least, I hope you remember the cheap chocolate advent calendars we bring home from the grocery store, and all the affiliated deal-making that spans the month of December:

"What if I have two chocolates today, Dad, and none tomorrow?"

"I'm just going to peek at Day 12, but I promise I won't eat it."

It feels impossible to be a good parent sometimes. Your mother and I say this constantly. For a long time, my main job just was to keep you from becoming dead, and now it's mostly to be around when you need me, and when I'm too hard on myself for being impatient with you or frustrated by how exhausted I feel, this is the mantra I tell myself:

I am showing up every day for my kids.

Yes, this is the third day in a row that you have insisted we try to make fresh mozzarella even though it appears to be impossible to end up with anything but a gelatinous mess, but I'm doing it because encouraging your curiosity seems like the best way to connect, and also pass the many, many hours around the house before you eventually move out on your own. How we moved from picture books and Legos to assembling a computer to building an acrobatic drone to mastering the Rubik's Cube to attempting homemade salt water taffy and now gourmet cheese is something of a mystery to me, but each day brings new enthusiasms, usually by way of you buried under your covers watching a DIY YouTube channel.

Yesterday, you mentioned wanting to take up welding and/or skydiving, and I said no—I have my limits, although sometimes I wonder if my judgment is faulty. A month ago, my iPhone wasn't working properly and you said, "Let's fix it," and I said, "No way, too complicated." But you wore me down, as is your habit, and the next thing I knew we've ordered parts on the internet and my phone is in hundreds of pieces on the dining room table with screws the size of rice grains stuck to masking tape so they don't roll away, and by the evening of the first day, we were both in despair. I put you to bed, and you started crying, and saying how sorry you were that my phone was destroyed. And some patron saint of good fatherliness inhabited my body at that moment because I comforted you and said, "It's not your fault. We took this on together, and if we can't fix it, then

I'll just get another phone and we'll chalk this up to a great adventure." And then I went to bed furious that I hadn't just taken the damn phone to be repaired by professionals, that my shitty judgment was not only going to cost me $700, but had led you to feel so guilty and miserable on my behalf. But then the next afternoon, both of us back from school, we started in again around the dining room table, and a few hours later, I pushed the power button on the reassembled phone, and the look on your face when that white Apple logo appeared on the screen made the whole miserable escapade worth it.

It doesn't always turn out right.

Like the time you let me fly your drone, and I lost control, and I flew it over the neighborhood school, crashing it just as Back-to-School Night was letting out. By some cosmic act of mercy, it didn't hit anyone, but we were both traumatized. And how heartbroken I was when weeks later, you told me that every time you closed your eyes to fall asleep, you saw the drone plummeting out of the sky. I insisted we fix it, and go back to the school grounds so you could replace that horrible event with happier, newer memories, and we did, but your enthusiasm for flying the drone never really returned.

That one's on me.

My father didn't do drones or mozzarella or even teach me to pound a nail. I was only slightly older than you are as I write this when he stopped parenting completely. Once my parents divorced, I went to boarding school in India, and then after a year moved back to the U.S. with my mother, and that was the last time my father and I ever spent time together under the same roof. And mostly I didn't mind. We both probably felt a good deal of relief that we didn't have to navigate the complexities of father/son anymore.

But later, when I was in my twenties, I did wish it could have been different. My father didn't leave me a letter that starts with, "If you're reading this, it's because I'm dead" and maybe this letter is just one more iteration of me telling you, "I love you"—an insurance policy in case you ever doubt or forget it once I'm gone; or maybe it's the artifact of the letter itself—me wishing that my dad had intentionally left something of value specifically for me.

Full disclosure: I do have two brass goblets from Nepal that he once gave me—part of a failed business venture that he concocted. I guess he thought there would be a big market in the U.S. for Nepalese brass goblets and bowls and things, but Americans have always preferred plastic stuff from China, so he ended up with hundreds of these items that he eventually gave away to anyone who would take some. I just hope my two goblets don't fall off their high shelf because they could kill someone they're so heavy.

A writing prompt/thought experiment I once gave my high school students: Imagine standing in a field, say, or on an empty basketball court, and somehow magically all the things you ever owned appear laid out before you. Every pair of socks, every toy, that favorite pen with the feather on the end, (my first piece of knitting that someone stole from me in the second grade in New Zealand that I cried about for a week), baby teeth, cash . . . what memories would surface that might otherwise have been forever lost to you? How many objects might you not remember ever owning at all? Sometimes I wish I could go back and browse through it all.

One happy object from my childhood that is lost now: we used to go to the beach in Thailand for the Christmas holiday, and one year my parents got me a Walkman—this was when they first came out and were the size of a brick—and I'd buy bootlegged cassette tapes on the streets of Bangkok, hefting the Walkman around with me everywhere I went, listening to Bruce Springsteen or Rush. Then again, that might have been the same holiday that my parents thought it would be a good idea to let my brother and me take a taxi to Pat Pong, an area of Bangkok where tourists pick up prostitutes. We walked from bar to bar looking at all the girls with numbers on their bathing suits, watching drunk tourists choose their prey. Even then, I remember wondering about my parents' judgment letting us go down there by ourselves. The girls all pinched my cheeks and laughed at what a baby I was. Which was ironic, because many of the girls were barely older than me. But the Walkman was amazing. I can still perfectly picture its silver case and black buttons.

My most sincere wish in all this world is that I will be a good father to you and your sister, and we remain close for all my days on this earth.

Is that too much to ask?

Have I done something stupid to drive you away years down the line?

Have you pushed me away?

Other than losing you altogether, these are my worst fears. Parenting you is not always a lot of fun, which at first glance might seem contradictory to my deepest wish of being a good father, since there are so many moments in any given day that I honestly don't feel like parenting at all. Often, I would prefer to read, or take a walk with your mom, or nap, watch Netflix, or just be left alone to stare out the window—but you and your sister are far too needy to give your mother and me much of that. There is always a trip to Home Depot to gather the necessary components to make a bow and arrow out of PVC pipe, or we're just pleading with you to wear a coat, eat your dinner, wash your feet, don't go to sleep with your shoes on.

Despite all of the irritations, inconveniences, costs, and demands you two impose on us, our love for you both burns with an intensity that eclipses all else in our lives. In other words, there is nothing else in the universe with the same capacity to make us as abjectly miserable and insecure. Will any of this resonate with you now, if you have children of your own who are driving you half-nuts? Sweet revenge, if so.

I will have to resist the urge to revise this letter many years from now if my life somehow goes off the rails—divorce, destitution, cancer, environmental collapse. No, just accept these words as evidence of a particular moment; if nothing else, the time when your mother and I sensed our own mortality and gave too much money to a lawyer for a fancy will in a padded three-ring binder that happened to have an empty section labeled "Personal Information".

In other words, a snapshot of when life was still mostly good.

Or maybe I'll add to the letter as my life progresses, so by the time of my demise it will be several volumes, and you'll just skip right to the last couple paragraphs when I'm ranting about pink bunnies taking over the moon.

Dash is at my feet. Can I admit I am struggling to love this dog? I know the rest of the family does, and despite my reservations about getting him, I relented only because your sister waged a two-year campaign of acting like she would die if we didn't get a little dog. Do you remember all this? The trip an hour north to choose him from that litter of puppies on the farm with the alpacas just up the road from the industrial cattle farm—the stench of that place!—and then the moment when both you and your sister agreed on the same puppy, which seemed like a miracle given you rarely agree on anything; the drive back when he threw up in the car, and then, of course, the daily grind of taking care of him, and wiping his piss off the floor with paper towels, and now he destroys my beloved backyard garden with such tail-wagging enthusiasm.

Would I be sad if this dog ran away and never came back? I would be sad for all of you, of course; I would comfort you all with the intensity of a saint, but I fear the energy for that consolation would be coming not from shared grief, but from pure, hidden exultation. No, I hate the barking, and the smell of the creature, and my constant recriminations towards him to behave, and get down, and I loathe

the way he follows me around the house wanting something that I can't give. I know people love dogs because they are such reliable companions and their love is unconditional, but I just resent the dog for that. I feel as if I never have enough of what the dog needs: affection, patience, attention, and the reason is that I have given it all to you and your sister, or my students, or your mom, and there just isn't any left for the fucking dog.

The other day, I was taking him for a walk, and I passed a woman with her dog, and while the dogs sniffed each other's butts, she excitedly asked me about Dash—his breed and age, etc.—and it was so clear she thought that I loved my dog as much as she loved hers, and I wanted to say to her, "I am not the kind of person you think I am."

I had dogs as a kid in Nepal—three of them in fact, near identical, one after the other because the larger dog next door killed the first two by jumping over the wall and snapping their necks. This was in Kathmandu, where dogs were not revered as they are here, although people did have them as pets and fed them scraps. I was inconsolable after the deaths of the first two, but then we moved to a different part of town, and the third identical dog lived to a ripe old age, although we ultimately left Nepal and the dog behind.

Is that the story that psychologically explains why I don't love Dash as much as I should?

I'm thinking again of when my father died and of some of his things I found in his house: an address book filled with names and scraps of paper he'd scribbled on for most of his adult life. The book was so overstuffed, he held it together with rubber bands; a leather-bound journal he wrote in when he was younger. I have these books here with me now in the studio on a shelf—the same one on which I am displaying his ugly brass goblets. How strange that things like scrawled driving directions on a piece of Embassy Suites stationery can outlast the man himself—it's hard to reconcile the fact that mundane and unimportant objects have more permanence than we do. But isn't that also the very point of these words that I am writing? That you will find them once I am gone?

I was an avid journal writer myself in my twenties. Are those thirty-odd volumes still around? They're here with me now on the shelf, but who knows where they will have ended up by the time you read this. Assuming you find them, this seems as good a moment as any to tell you to please feel free to do whatever you want with the books—burn them, study them for clues to my essential character, pass them down unread to your own children as an artifact of how the world used to be. Unless they are somehow destroyed (and the whole world does seem to be going up in flames, lately), I'm not sure I will ever have the heart to dispose of them. I was grateful to find my father's journal. I couldn't read it at first, not for a couple of years after he died, but there was a period of time when I stopped being able to sleep. Every night, I would feel myself begin to drift off, then jerk awake with a gasp of breath. I couldn't make sense of it, and worried that I had the beginning symptoms of some horrible neurological disease. Eventually, after maybe a month of this, I went to an acupuncturist a friend recommended, and after looking at my tongue and taking my pulse, and after putting needles in several key points on my body, the doctor diagnosed me with grief, and indeed I began to sob right there on the table, and after weeks of intermittent sobbing and further acupuncture treatments, I returned to the land of living by day and sleeping at night.

This is all to say that when I die, grieve for as long and hard as necessary. Otherwise, you will poison yourself. I thought I grieved my father because I wrote and published an essay about the days leading up to and following his death—and it was hard to write, and I cried sometimes while completing it—but apparently the universe deemed publication insufficient. Life sought its recompense, and I wouldn't wish that kind of insomnia on my worst enemy. So wail and weep and see firsthand that there's nothing to fear from expressing all that emotion. And if it doesn't come right away, be patient and allow it to manifest however it chooses—just know that no one escapes, not even you with that giant brain of yours.

It was during that time, after I had emerged from the storm of insomnia, when I summoned the courage to read little bits of his journal. He wrote his first entry on January 1st, 1959 with this proclamation: *Being nineteen years old, I think it's time that I begin to become a man. For several years now I have wandered aimlessly through the catacombs of my thoughts without settling on any manly goals. The time has come to begin to build a foundation of wisdom.* He wrote in the journal intermittently for exactly four years, the last short entry on January 1st, 1963, which reads, *New Year's Eve. Terrible cold for three days then a party.* He never wrote in it again, which is remarkable because he kept the journal with him his whole life, across how many countries and continents and three marriages. Maybe he kept it for his kids to find. Maybe it reminded him of the person he once sought to become. I've been trying to write things all my life, so I felt a pang of recognition and empathy for his lofty, ambitious beginning and then the inevitable letdown of his abrupt and banal ending.

I fully realize from reading his journal that it's weird and uncomfortable to feel around inside your parent's head, but doing so helped me face the reality that he was gone, that an individual man once roamed the earth and then was no more, if that makes any sense. So I was grateful for the journal, and I guess what I'm hoping is that this letter and maybe all my own journals might help you someday process that I was fully alive before I was gone.

It is too bad that as children, we do not often have the capacity to meet our parents on their own terms. If the whole enterprise is working properly, perhaps this is as it should be. But the consequence is that we forfeit knowing our parents in certain crucial ways, and it's only once they are gone do we realize how selfish we were, and wish we'd had more perspective. The other day you were mean and short with your mom, and later, after she had rightly banished you to your room, she said to me, "It's better that they're assholes with us, and not their teachers or their friends." And she's right about that. Perhaps we can reassure ourselves we're doing a good job as parents when our presence and goodwill is taken for granted to a large degree, hard as it is not to take it personally sometimes.

Does this all feel like too much?

You can stop reading this letter right now if you like.

Fine by me—I'm done and gone.

No pressure at all.

But thanks for reading. I know you're probably very busy.

Unfortunately, despite my father's youthful wish for wisdom, he did not become wise about how to parent his children. He abdicated that responsibility almost completely. Most likely, you barely remember him now, if at all. I asked you about him recently and you said you remembered us going to a park for a picnic and my dad showed you how to open a bottle of champagne, and I laughed because almost surely that never happened. My father did not picnic and he did not drink champagne, but maybe my memory of him is as unreliable as yours. Nevertheless, if that's your only memory of him, I'm glad it's a happy one— no matter that I'm pretty sure you're confusing him with someone else.

As I continued to read entries in his journal, I was struck by how much I didn't know about his early life, and except for a couple of occasions, I never really asked for details. Would I have felt more of a connection with him if I could have known more about the forces that shaped him as a young man? He was complicated, and he did cause me considerable emotional pain while growing up—mostly by just not being around much, or having to navigate his mercurial mood swings when he was around— but he lived a rich, interesting life all the same, and it gives me some solace to know he was trying to be a good person. The journal is proof that despite his failings, my father had a good heart, and he wanted to know himself.

Maybe the 10,000 pages of journal entries from my twenties are ample evidence of my early life. It's all in there: the loves, the loneliness, the earnest attempts to know myself and carve out a small piece of the world that I could call my own. As a reader, a journal is a window into another person; as a writer, it's a window into knowing ourselves. If there's one single thing that helped me know myself better, it would be journaling all those years. I was not lying to myself—just a pen and notebook—figuring out what I was feeling, and how to be with myself. Of course, you don't have to journal to be honest with yourself, but for me it has always been the easiest way to do it: to run a thought or a feeling or an idea to its source and see what it looks like on paper, outside the tumult of my mind. The process of journaling by its very nature of revelation ought to make anyone a more empathic person. Plus, you just feel less bottled up. Repressed emotion or anger or frustration will always make you more likely to behave recklessly, or at the very least, less capable of seeing the world from someone's perspective other than your own.

Inevitably, you will be cruel sometimes; you will be unkind, and act selfishly, and not have clear answers for many things. People will want things from you that you cannot give; you will want things from others they are incapable of giving. There's a lot of hurt to be doled out and received in life, and on many levels most things do not go exactly the way we wish. Journaling has always been my way through the storm, and if I have emerged on the other side less likely to blow up my own life, less likely to harm another person, I have journaling every day for ten years to thank for it.

Of course, self-awareness certainly doesn't always make the moment to moment of parenting feel any easier—less enraging or confounding or wishing for clearer answers on the best consequence or course of action. Case in point: towards the end of this past summer, your mother and I tried to get you to wear your swim shirt before leaving the house for a pool party.

Do you remember that?

You refused, saying you'd put it on when you got there. Driving you to the party with your buddy in the car (already in *his* swim attire, I must add), you were treating me like I was the dumbest dad alive. Yes, I was confused about the location of the party, and yes, it might have seemed ridiculous and embarrassing that I was still confused even after we'd pulled up next to the balloons fluttering in the breeze, but did you have to be such a little shit about it? I was convinced your derision was somehow connected to showing off for your friend, so as we walked towards the party, I pulled you aside—*you're acting like a spoiled brat*, I said—and you huffed away to join your friends. Because I was so angry (and relieved, really) to be rid of you for a couple hours, I forgot to insist one more time that you put your swim shirt on.

The result was second-degree burns on your shoulders and back. Great puffy blisters that burst and oozed yellow goo. That was the first time I can remember being so angry at you for so many consecutive hours. And worried too. Worried sick about what you'd done to yourself. The next day, we decided your mother would stay behind with you on our vacation week because you could barely move without screaming in agony. After your sister and I left for the trip, your mother took you to the doctor where they wrapped you in some kind of antibiotic second skin. That whole eight-hour drive to southern Utah, I was boiling with a toxic combination of rage and concern—wondering mile after flat mile if it was possible to teach your children anything at all. Is it some nonsensical, evolutionarily advantageous trait that children always resist the good advice of their parents?

And I'm scared because you're only about to turn eleven. What's coming down the pike? I often hear my high school students saying stuff like, "My parents are so pissed off at me right now," or "My parents can't even speak to me they're so angry," and I just assume this is some deficiency in their parenting, like they don't have enough love and forgiveness in their hearts to connect with their own kids. But I get it now: our kids, the very creatures we are biologically hardwired to protect, sometimes insist on behaving like stupid assholes.

So, maybe this letter is nothing but a prayer that you've made it safely into adulthood. When I spoke to you on the phone from Utah, after the nurses had scraped away some of the dead skin and oozing pustules, you cried for a moment and said, "I love you, Dad," and all my frustration fell away in an instant, and I just wanted to cradle you in my arms. As your parent, I am yoked to you forever.

My need of you is surely greater than your need of me—another painful paradox that I must come to terms with as I watch you becoming increasingly independent. It is impossible to keep you entirely safe, I know that. You will do stupid things, and no advice from me is going to change that.

But I do hope that you wear sunscreen now.

Have they blocked out the sun with a giant orbiting umbrella to try and drop the soaring temperatures?

Can you even go outside anymore?

How bad is it nowadays?

Are you holed up in some underground bunker, eating protein paste from tubes?

A strange thing happened when I was so furious with you over The Sunscreen Incident: I realized it was okay to be really angry at your kid sometimes. That maybe it doesn't jeopardize your relationship for them to see your pain and frustration and maddening concern. I say this because I so vividly remember the times my father was out of control with anger, the times he spanked me hard, his strength terrifying. He was not ordinarily prone to violence and rage—on the contrary, he was actually a gentle man in most ways—but he was also a diabetic, and in those days, it was harder to treat diabetes with the consistency that electronic insulin pumps now ensure. He would occasionally get dangerously low blood sugar, become irrational and physically erratic. Some memories will never leave me—my mother sending us kids to our rooms for our own protection as she would chase my father around the house with a spoonful of honey as he stumbled and raged like a toddler. Children don't forget such things, and maybe that is the single biggest reason I never bonded with my father properly.

But perhaps with you, I have gone too far in the opposite direction. Because I am so determined to never traumatize you, I also never allow myself to be really angry, to communicate in a visceral and raw way, my frustration and disappointment in your behavior. But the sunscreen incident proved I was wrong about that, and as you move forward into adolescence, I am glad I know that now, because god only knows what you'll get up to in the next few years that will send me over the edge.

My father's rage terrified me, mostly because he was not in control. It was as if he became possessed by a demon, and I didn't understand how one person could become another person like that. Once, when

I was in my twenties and he was camping up in northern Vermont, I went to visit him for a weekend, and it rained the whole time, so we mostly sat in his tiny trailer. I was hoping for a deeper connection with my dad at that point in my life—lonely, writing feverishly in those journals every day—and maybe because I was feeling so wretched, I felt braver about opening up to him. I remember asking him about his parents, and he told me how strict they were and that when his mother died, he never cried. I didn't understand him at first, so I asked again and he said, yes, he'd never cried one time in his whole life about losing his mother. My father never allowed himself to grieve for her.

This shocked me. And at that moment, I thought I understood where his rage came from, and why he couldn't let himself be vulnerable enough to parent properly. Sitting in that rainy, god-forsaken trailer, I decided that it wasn't the diabetes, or at least not all of it. No, his choice not to grieve his mother was how he short-circuited the emotional pathways in his brain. Who knows if this is true, but it's the story that makes the most sense to me, the only thing that makes a plausible reason for how someone as smart and sensitive as my father could abandon parenting his children.

And so two years after he died, I properly grieved my father. It wasn't easy, but I did it. And when my mother dies, I will grieve her, and it will probably hurt far worse because I have been close to her my whole life. She made up for my father's absence and then some.

And now you must grieve me, and maybe this letter will help.

What is left to tell you? I realize I have not said much about so many things, so many places. Again, that nagging uncertainty of what is the right amount to tell? What things might you wish to know that you probably never asked me about?

My first date? Too cliché? Her name was B. and she was tall, blond, and German. We were ten or eleven, and I really thought she was the one because just the weekend before we had sort of slow danced to Air Supply's *All Out of Love* at the school dance. This was in Kathmandu, and there was a small movie theatre that was part of a compound for westerners (think tennis courts, snack bar, swimming pool); one of our parents dropped us off to see *Superman*, which was a big deal because we had to wait years to see movies after they were released in the U.S. She walked in front of me down the theatre aisle, and as she turned into a row, I hesitated—some part of my brain stopped working because I suddenly thought it would be too forward to actually sit next to her on our date. I scooted down the row directly behind her instead, and as Superman flew backward around the world, I let her sumptuous, blond locks touch my knees, and I hoped that she would register this as a sign of our deep connection. It was our only date. She went on to become a helicopter pilot for the army.

Or how about Christian missionary boarding school in India? At boarding school, everything worthwhile happened in "the cud." The school sat on a series of ridges, mountains dropping off on both sides into steep wilderness, and we called these slopes "the cud," an area where teachers, dormitory parents, and perhaps even God never went. The kids owned the cud, and the cud was the reason most of my formative sexual experiences that year were achieved on a slant. I wanted to be like R., an upperclassman, the most handsome and sophisticated man I had ever met: chiseled jawline, eyes the size of chapatis (Indian tortillas), stinky French cologne, immaculate clothes. He dated the most beautiful girl in the school, of course, Y., who was half-Indian, half-Austrian, a combination that left anyone in her vicinity looking like week-old rice. I had two roommates, V., a pudgy straight-laced kid from Saudi Arabia who wanted to be a doctor, and D., an American like me, who was a pot-head. There was no privacy— us ninth grade boys showered together, shat together (the toilets were just lined up in a row), ate the terrible dormitory food together, and took care of our adolescent urges together. And if you ever did have a moment alone, be careful, because God was always watching. The Lord hung over that school like a wet, wool blanket and the cud was the only place I ever felt like I could be myself. My roommate, D., was kicked out halfway through the year after a room raid because the dormitory proctors found his stash. I'd given up pot the year before since I had basically flunked out of school in Nepal, but smoked cigarettes every opportunity I could get, and hid them successfully in the ripped lining of my winter coat.

I became a master manipulator that year. My dormitory parents—a young missionary couple—loved me because I often babysat their one-year-old daughter, and once I saved her from being bitten by a scorpion. She was leaning down to pick it up, and I saw it just in time and pulverized it with my foot. Scorpions were everywhere. We checked our beds for them every night before climbing in to sin against ourselves. Anyway, they loved me, those house-parents. They never suspected I was off in the cud smoking and feeling up girls. Sometimes I'd go to their little apartment on the first floor of the dormitory for afternoon tea. I'd sit politely and say things like, "Sometimes I can feel God is talking to me." They'd pull out their Bibles and would discuss the glories of the Lord while I sat there eating hand-fuls of cookies, a serious and inquisitive look on my face. It was a double life and it served me well at the time, keeping me out of trouble and affording me certain latitudes the "bad kids" were not given, like dropping down into the cud so I could sin.

Early on in my year there, I convinced everyone I was a Buddhist. I did this partly because it annoyed the shit out of the missionaries, whose main purpose in life was to bring you into the loving arms of Christ, but also because as long as you had a faith of *some* kind, they mostly left you alone. If you didn't have any religion, watch out, because they'd swoop down and stuff you full of Jesus. Pretending to be a Buddhist served me in other ways too. Just before lights out in the dormitory when the proctors would sweep through the rooms making sure everything was copacetic, I'd light incense and do prostrations to Buddha, chanting "Om mane padme om." I timed this perfectly, the room filling up with incense smoke just as the proctors would pop their heads in yelling, "Lights out!" and I'd finish up my chanting, shut the door, kill the lights, and smoke a leisurely cigarette before climbing into bed to sin against myself. That was boarding school in India. After a year, with my parents newly divorced, my mother decided to move us to America.

Tell me about the circus, you ask? At work sometimes, I show my students a picture of me as a clown from the Ringling Brothers glossy color program that year (this was 1990) and they can't reconcile the balding middle-aged man they know with the eighteen-year-old purple-wigged, red-nosed kid in the picture. They laugh and take photos of the photo with their phones and post them on Instagram or god-knows-where else with the caption, "Holy shit! That's Mr. Kaplan!" And who can blame them? They pepper me with questions, but only against the backdrop of their own expectations. In other words, no one—students and grown-ups alike—expects to hear anything that strays too far from what they already imagine, and I almost always oblige with short and clever answers:

Did you climb out of the little car? (Yes, dressed in a monkey suit.)

Did you make a lot of money? (173 dollars a week)

Did they abuse the animals? (No. They preferred abusing the clowns.)

Mostly, I avoid the truth: the circus was a crash course in dysfunction. How alcoholism, domestic violence, isolation, poverty, lack of education, and strict social hierarchies can limit people's lives in powerful ways. For a year, traveling and living on the circus train, I saw the underbelly of American life. And I was a kid who had only recently returned from spending my childhood in developing countries, and still I was shocked at how raw so much of American life was. I almost quit the show several times, mostly because of complicated interpersonal dynamics: a fellow clown who became disturbingly obsessed with me, and when I confronted him and told him I couldn't like him "like that" he grew belligerent and incensed that I was accusing him of being gay—yet another type of rage due to lack of self-awareness. Or the young Romanian acrobat I befriended, and when her uncle found out that we were exchanging notes, he pinned me up against a wall and told me he would kill me if I didn't stop.

I believed him. And from that moment on until the day I left the show, I was afraid.

No one much wants to hear these types of stories. Which is why I have the easier answers ready to go.

Did you really live on the circus train? (Yes, and it was a mile long, most of the space reserved for the elephants.)

When I left the circus for the leafy tranquility of Lewis and Clark College in Portland, Oregon, it felt like another continental divide, as dramatic as leaving India behind for Vermont. When Ringling Brothers circus finally closed permanently a few years ago, people asked me if I was sad about that, and the answer is no. Some things should come to an end, and that circus was one of them.

Tomorrow you turn eleven, and the anniversary of your birth reminds me of this long and mostly happy chapter in my life. I'm dreading the events of your birthday celebration—could anything be worse than spending twenty-four hours at a water park hotel?—but I have learned mostly to keep the dread to myself. I have to be careful around birthdays. Once years ago, we were having your party at a gymnastics center, and I was so grumpy gathering all the party stuff into the car that your mother turned on me and yelled, "So don't come then!" and she meant it.

Ironically, I met your mother at a birthday party for a mutual friend in New York City sixteen years ago— a party that I almost didn't attend because I hate birthday parties so much.

Can you imagine?

How terrifying that so much happiness and meaning can unfold from a simple decision to attend a birthday party.

But here we are.

You and your sister and your mother are the great saviors of my adult life.

And I'm even coming around with Dash. He will turn one soon, and week-by-week I feel my resistance waning. Not love exactly, but when he looks up at me now, I can see a soul in there. He is no longer just *creature*, but rather *our creature*. I still hate the barking, and will never let him lick my face, but I don't wish him gone either. My fantasy that he run away so I can be Consoler-in-Chief is appalling. I see the joy he brings all of you, and like the day we spent at the water-park hotel, sometimes that has to be enough.

How to end this letter?

Impossible because I cannot imagine ever having to say goodbye to you.

I cannot bear the thought.

So I will duck and divert.

How about a list of 47 things a good man should be able to do around the house—one for each year I have been alive? Some of these you have already mastered at age eleven, and some are a work in progress (#3). I can hear you arguing the virtues of several already (#5, 9, and 12), which is how I know you are my son.

Here goes: If the world is still recognizable, and domestic human life is still intact, I sincerely hope you have learned to:

1. Clean a toilet

2. Unclog a toilet

3. Wipe your own pee off a toilet

4. Change a flat tire

5. Write thank-you cards

6. Put a chain back on a bicycle

7. Hug another man without feeling weird about it

8. Hug another man and if you feel like doing more than hugging, acknowledge that fact to yourself and be okay with it

9. Follow directions

10. Unclog a garbage disposal

11. Put your hand in a garbage disposal and pretend you turned it on by accident

12. Plant things

13. Water things

14. Prune things

15. Cook a variety of foods and don't make an ungodly mess while doing it

16. Talk difficult things out

17. Argue when necessary

18. Apologize

19. Forgive

20. Not expect perfection. Good-enough is fine most of the time, especially with cooking, cleaning, laundry, yard work, and sex

21. Hang a picture on a wall
22. Converse easily with a variety of people who come to visit
23. Know when you need a hug and ask for one
24. Know when someone else needs a hug and give one
25. Know when you need to cry, and cry
26. Ask for help lifting heavy things
27. Make a good omelet
28. Kill small things without fussing, such as flies and spiders
29. Clean hair out of a drain
30. Run your own home finances
31. Know when to call the professionals
32. This includes a psychologist
33. Manage your passwords effectively
34. Have friendly chats with your neighbors
35. Maintain friendships
36. Retain the ability to touch your toes
37. Un-jamb things—staplers, printers, windows, drawers, relationships

38. Say no politely, but without apology to door-to-door salespeople
39. Engage children in conversation
40. Express your doubts, fears, frustrations, joys, and insecurities
41. Dig a hole
42. Bury a pet
43. Grieve a pet
44. Grieve a parent
45. Bury a parent (not at home)
46. Make a decent vinaigrette
47. Get enough sleep

I love you.
A thousand times I love you, boy of mine. . .

Your Father

Acknowledgments

Thank you to Leslie M. Browning and Homebound Publications for believing in this project and so beautifully bringing it to life. To Stephen Trimble for his great advice and mentorship. To my Creative Writing students at Denver School of the Arts for their fearless work and believing in the power of books. To my mom for her perspective, humor, and lifelong encouragement. To Anne, Toby, and Molly for sharing their lives with me and making our home such a special place. To all parents everywhere, who do the hardest work there is.